# THE NATIONAL POETRY SERIES

*The National Poetry Series* was established in 1978 to ensure the
publication of five poetry books annually through five participating
publishers. Publication is funded annually by the Lannan Foundation,
Amazon Literary Partnership, Barnes & Noble, The Poetry Foundation,
The PG Family Foundation and The Betsy Community Fund,
Joan Bingham, Mariana Cook, Stephen Graham, Juliet Lea Hillman
Simonds, William Kistler, Jeffrey Ravetch, Laura Baudo Sillerman,
and Margaret Thornton. For a complete listing of generous contributors to
The National Poetry Series, please visit www.nationalpoetryseries.org.

2014 Competition Winners

*Monograph*
by Simeon Berry of Somerville, Massachusetts
Chosen by Denise Duhamel for University of Georgia Press

*The Regret Histories*
by Joshua Poteat of Richmond, Virginia
Chosen by Campbell McGrath for HarperCollins

*Let's Let That Are Not Yet : Inferno*
by Ed Pavlić of Athens, Georgia
Chosen by John Keene for Fence Books

*Double Jinx*
by Nancy Reddy of Madison, Wisconsin
Chosen by Alex Lemon for Milkweed Editions

*Viability*
by Sarah Vap of Venice, California
Chosen by Mary Jo Bang for Penguin Books

MONOGRAPH

# monograph

poems by simeon berry

THE UNIVERSITY OF GEORGIA PRESS  *athens & london*

© 2015 by the University of Georgia Press
Athens, Georgia 30602
www.ugapress.org
All rights reserved
Set in Garamond Premier Pro
Printed and bound by Sheridan Books
The paper in this book meets the guidelines for
permanence and durability of the Committee on
Production Guidelines for Book Longevity of the
Council on Library Resources.

Most University of Georgia Press titles are
available from popular e-book vendors.

Printed in the United States of America

15  16  17  18  19  P  5  4  3  2  1

Library of Congress Cataloging-in-Publication Data

Berry, Simeon, author.
[Poems. Selections]
Monograph / Poems by Simeon Berry.
pages cm — (The National Poetry Series)
ISBN 978-0-8203-4845-2 (pbk. : alk. paper) — ISBN 978-0-8203-4846-9 (ebook)
I. Title.
PS3602.E76385A6 2015
811'.6—dc23
2014047578
British Library Cataloging-in-Publication Data available

*For H., J., and L.*

A monogram is a symbol of a person's identity, usually made up of initials. A monograph is a treatise or detailed study of one relatively narrow topic.

—*The Columbia Guide to Standard American English* (1993)

The indirect means of arousal which are possible through words need not be dwelt upon here at length.

—C.K. Ogden and I. A. Richards, *The Meaning of Meaning*

# Contents

# i. contra preferentum

Thought back to that first
October after moving to the city.
Both of us temping. Broke and
in debt. Barely able to afford the
rent on a basement efficiency
next to the elevator. Our sole
extravagance a bonsai tree stiff-
ening on the window.

Fairly certain we were
doomed as a couple. Repeating
this to myself every night as I
walked home in darkness through
the close, suburban streets, the
smell of the sea infiltrating the
fog. Utterly ecstatic with rage.

When my grandfather tried to tell my dad obliquely that my mother was mentally ill, he had to take him out on the water in his rowboat to do it.

There they were safe. Or at least equally in danger. He—like other New England fishermen— could not swim. These are the people I come from.

R. says C. has been dredging up a bunch of sexual trauma. This is the second girl he's dated who was raped in the past.

Last night, he came home stoned. C. was enraged, and when he turned his back on her, she punched him.

He just said, *I can't believe you did that,* then walked away.

She rushed after him, shouting, *Wait! Don't you want to know why I hit you?*

There is a principle in contract law called *contra preferentum*—any ambiguity in a document shall be construed against the drafter of the document. In poetry, this is reversed.

At the end of that first evening, N. scrawls her number on the back of her business card and gives it to me.

When I turn it over, I see what she's listed under her name: *Cartographer ~ Demolitionist.*

I am incredibly envious. I look up at her, and she raises an eyebrow. *Well? Which do you require?*

When my dad was traveling and teaching healing in Europe, he woke in his hotel one morning and discovered that his passport was missing.

The room was full of spirit guides arguing about where he should go next. As soon as he yelled at them they vanished, and the passport instantly appeared right in front of him on the nightstand.

These kinds of ambiguous difficulties are not, as they say, in the literature. But they're what make this real for me.

If I took one thing from my father's universe, it's that everyone has an agenda, even when they don't have a body.

As soon as N. moves in with me, her best friend visits. *Her wife,* as they term it.

The first afternoon, I come home from editing the magazine to find the friend smirking and lying topless on the sofa in N.'s arms. She has very boring breasts.

N. doesn't seem to be particularly engaged, but she doesn't object either. *Now here,* I think, *is a challenge.*

Yet I am not upset—at least not until later that night at the grad school poetry reading, when N. sits between us in the front row and holds both our hands.

Even though someone is reciting couplets about wisteria and sperm in a college auditorium, it's still my place of business.

I am eventually compelled to admit that this is silly. My *brain* is my place of business.

# II. performance art

Months later, the topless friend tries to break my ankle by demonstrating how not to do a dance move.

I forgive her, for the simple reason that every night I get to fuck N., while all she can do is write poems entitled *The Loss to the Heterosexual Dream.*

N. asks me to tie her to a cold radiator, while the friend handles enjambment badly. Later on, the differences will seem less dramatic.

When Raymond Chandler was teaching himself how to write, he could barely get his hero to set down his hat in a convincing manner. It was years before he could gracefully get a character out of a room.

This is why I don't write prose. I hate choreography. Just fill up the bong with Delphic smoke, please, and I'll find a way to get out of the stanza. See? Like that.

N.'s favorite film is the documentary *Sans Soleil,* which begins with a dark screen and an unknown female narrator:

*The first image he told me about was of three children on a road in Iceland in 1965.*

We get a brief glimpse of this footage, and then she adds:

*He wrote me: One day I'll have to put it all alone at the beginning of a film. . . . If they don't see happiness in the picture, at least they'll see the black.*

The whole movie is like this: brilliant, disconnected, alternately pretentious and naively amazed, continuously telling you what it's doing *as* it's doing it.

N. thinks the film is real, but the director isn't. Or the director's transparent, but the work is wholly artificial.

There's no equivalent of a dark screen on the page, so—if you would—please see every white space as black.

N. told me she trained herself to masturbate with highlighters. First one, then two, then three. It was her reward for homework.

I cannot imagine she thought I would be able to resist lingering over this metaphor.

How French to make scholarship seem sexy. How American to make the emphasis literal.

For weeks, I toy with the idea of writing an essay comparing performance art to pornography.

The only time either form feels remotely genuine or unique is when something goes wrong.

Both owe a lot to medieval martyrs. Either the performers suffer or the audience suffers from what it's forced to watch. But *someone* has to suffer.

N. is very protective of performance artists, so she gets upset whenever I gleefully reason out another link. It doesn't stop me, but it does make me want to kiss her.

I told N. that what sealed the deal for me was her favorite lines of poetry: *I became a criminal when I fell in love. / Before that I was a waitress.*

Of course, it didn't hurt that she was notorious among our friends for having written a one-woman show about Emma Goldman with lots of noncanonical sex and full-frontal nudity.

She said that she was initially attracted to me because I had *a great skull for a smoking jacket.*

*Well,* I said, *someone had to.*

# III. uniforms

When I was born, I weighed 8
pounds. Twelve months later, I was
back down to my birth weight and
dying.

During this year, my mother
wore jeans every day. The same pair of
jeans.

Clearly, she did not want to be
recognized as anything other than
a depressed person. There are worse
uniforms, I suppose.

In Genesis, any reference to Adam as a man is arguably wrong, at least until Eve.

The most accurate translation of the Hebrew word *ha'adam*, according to Phyllis Trible, is *earth creature* (from *ha,* humankind, and *adama,* earth). It is gender neutral.

As Sherry Simon writes, *Man and woman were given sexualized identities at the same time—and not one as a consequence of the other's existence.* This is a big deal. Why?

For one thing, it means that gender wars don't have to amount to mutually assured destruction.

Plus, I like thinking things are a big deal. I have to amuse myself somehow.

Isabella Stewart Gardiner placed a special clause in her will that required the paintings in her museum to be arranged exactly as she left them.

So when thieves cut the canvases out with knives, the empty frames had to remain on the wall. Now *that's* a contract with the reader.

N. said she didn't know she was a woman until she read Joan Didion's *sense of living one's deepest life underwater, that dark involvement with blood and birth and death*. . . .

I said that I didn't know I was an occultist until I read Dion Fortune on leaving the body:

> *There is no God of Israel to fight for him in battle and snuff up the savour of burnt offerings, but—there is a Logos, and the nature of the Logos can only be apprehended by those who can meditate in an empty shrine, that is to say, can think without a symbol.*

I said once you swallow that distinction, all the others are relatively meaningless.

We looked at each other. One of us had the wrong idea about what the other found exotic.

Compared notes with D. He has sex about three times a month, while I only have it twice a month.

He was cheerful: *Well, it sounds like your marriage is in a lot worse shape than mine!*

He is thinking of bugging his wife's computer, because he suspects she is cheating. She calls him drunk at 3 a.m. to ask him to come and pick her up from his friend's house.

He wishes—with a great deal of fervency—that he could confirm his suspicion that she was sexually abused as a child. It's all very East German.

Walked through the park last night with N. after going out for fancy, architectural desserts. Tiny chocolate reliquaries. Reductions and gels shaped into astrological crescents.

My suit made me feel mildly electrified, a subversive WASP who goes around leaving tweed explosives.

Fog ate the tops of the buildings and made the park smell like an ironworks.

N. pulled me underneath an oak and kissed me, saying mischievously, *If I were a sheep, you could legally graze me here on the Common. Moo.*

I was puzzled. *Moo?* She shook me by the shoulders gently. *Moo! How do you know I'm not a tiny cow in sheep's clothing?*

N.'s drama teacher said theater is like a glass of water. Mediocre actors will only get you partway to the top. You can fill up the rest with smoke, elaborate sets, and costumes.

Or you can have Elizabeth Taylor and Richard Burton in black turtlenecks, sitting in wooden chairs on a bare stage, and reading from a script.

I loved N.'s ultimate opinion about dictionary sex: when you walk away thinking, *I've just had sex.* This is the only tautology I've ever liked.

The night Woolf finally slept over, her lover, Vita Sackville-West, memorialized the event in her diary by simply writing three exclamation points.

I myself would want four, which demonstrates that the first thing one wants to do with a great metaphor is to wreck it.

# iv. sports

I seem to be terrible at certain religious differences, which irritates N. to no end. Apparently, *the Protestants are the ones who say all that shit after the Our Father* in the Lord's Prayer.

It sounds very informal, like sports, until the day I agree to go to Mass with her.

We're sitting at the end of the third pew when the priest starts to condemn gay marriage during his sermon.

N. stands up and—without changing her expression or looking back—walks out.

I am immensely proud of her, and we have a long, impassioned discussion about it. The next week, she goes back.

The first time I come home with N., her father and sister pick us up at the airport at night in a blizzard.

They have already opened a case of beer, and they all drink steadily during the harrowing drive back through the mountains.

I say nothing. I just think to myself, *Okay, so that's how it is.* . . . Later, I realize that this is *not* how it usually is. They were making a point.

A. says my guilt over disclosing these problems is silly. *All these things are open secrets.* *She wants you to feel like you're handing over the nuclear launch codes or something.*

She sighs into her tea. *In college, she didn't give a damn. There's nothing she wouldn't have said to anyone, no matter what the circumstances.*

A pause. *Of course, she also kissed girls, but that's not relevant to our purposes here.*

Decide to visit the historic sanitarium with Z., despite fighting with N. about it. She had no good explanation for why her crush on him has suddenly turned to hatred.

As Z. is trying to raise my spirits, a toddler wanders up beside us and points: *What's that?*

Her mother wearily replies: *That's a chair.* She pivots: *And that?* A sigh: *That's a table.* The child frowns: *Why?*

Z. smiles. *Miss, let me refer you to the collected works of Wittgenstein.*

N. asks what I want for my birthday, and nothing comes to mind, so I ask to be blindfolded.

She thinks about it for a few weeks, then consents.

I am tied to a chair, and, in the darkness, I hear her recite Kierkegaard and Hegel while she slowly reduces herself to lace and elastic and visits various pleasing depredations upon me.

The climax of the piece happens when she climbs on top of me and whispers in my ear:

*If.....it's......true.....that...........*
*....there.....are.....but....two.............*
*.......kinds.....of.....people.....in.........*
*.....this......world......the......logical.....*
*........positivists......and.......the..........*
*........goddamned........English........*
*....professors.....then.....I.....guess.........*
*......that....I....am....a....logical.........*
*....positivist.....*

I do not remind her that the only course I failed in college was Basic Symbolic Logic.

Often, right before sleep, N. would say, *Tell me a story*. And I would. I'd talk about quislings, secret underground rivers that flowed backwards, or why all the snowflakes in Hell are exactly alike.

I told hundreds of them, and she would almost always fall asleep before I finished. But, like Scheherazade, I found their loss pleasurable.

Until the night when we started having sex in the middle of one.

As soon as she suspected I was getting something out of them, they lost their appeal. They had to be pointless, or they'd just turn into art.

S. is working with a healer for her back, so she's dealing with her past lives.

She keeps apologizing for being *a crazy lady*, and I want to shield her with my body.

I tell her how—when I was a year old and dying—the angel in the shower told my dad where to find the clairvoyant who would diagnose and cure me in 48 hours with a Caycean course of treatment.

I tell her about watching my dad being taught healing when I was four.

I passed my hand over my younger brother in his crib. He turned bright red for a minute, and then his fever was gone.

I don't remember any of this, but I feel I should be covert about it.

Like I should mimic Philip Levine: talk openly about wrestling all night with an angel for his sick son's life, and then shut up about it and claim to be *about as mystical as a sofa*.

Return for the second half of Christmas with N.'s family. Overhear her father gloating to a friend on the phone about his lack of reaction when opening his presents: *You should have seen their little faces. So crestfallen.*

N. says he is difficult to shop for. I stare into my pallid eggnog as the plastic cup flexes in my hand.

The core of Anne Carson's *Eros the Bittersweet* is her analysis of why correspondence is erotic: because of the possibility that it might be intercepted.

This is analogous to how we talk about poems with *risk* in them— ultimately a dangerous metaphor. It tends to imply that the writer is the real victim here.

v. merit badges

Went out last night with M.
in a lavender tie and a purple shirt.
Felt like a sexual racketeer. Chandler
would have approved.

M. says he is fighting every
night with R., who is triumphantly
agoraphobic. They both scream and
cry and threaten to flee the apartment.
Then they have sex.

At first, I was frightened. Then
jealous. Then frightened again.

It is well to remember the chagrin of Leonard Cohen at such a time: *There are some people I know who think that there is nothing more important than making a song. Fortunately, this belief arises infrequently in their conversation.*

There are things I've done to make this story better. Some of them—the girl with the skull-and-crossbones hearing aid, the lover who got my joke about being able to speak Thieves' Cant—I did to others.

Some of them—my secret fetish for short hair, the Scandinavian film my life became—I did to myself.

I try but cannot resist secretly enjoying N.'s alarmed disapproval when my dad starts talking about *The Chronicles of Narnia*.

How the mythology is so heterogeneous and weird because C.S. Lewis attuned himself to the hybrid, pantheistic spirits of earth and space.

She has the same look I have observed when I emerge from the shower after belting out Protestant hymns.

Yes, a lot of my worldview happens outside the body.

But I quickly lose patience with the celestial merit badges of the New Agers.

And she doesn't understand how much I love the undertow in her Book. My Bible is the midnight version, the after-hours one. Where the beasts are attentive and the voices doubled, doubtful, alive.

N. confesses to me that she
watched *G.I. Joe* as a kid and that she
wanted to be Scarlett. (I myself loved
the mute, scarred Snake Eyes.)

I am dumbfounded. Even as a
ten-year-old, I found the show felt
unbelievably hokey. No one ever got
killed, and their M-16s fired dotted
lines of lasers, despite the fact that
they were clearly wearing belts of
ammunition.

At first I marvel over the irony.
I'm a pacifist who's never been in a
fight. She's a reformed radical lesbian.
Yet we like the same campy military
cartoon.

Then I get sad. This is what you
fall in love over.

Dreamed that a lot of people had been killed and buried in the sand.

Realized that this was Bloody Cove of my childhood, where a bunch of Native Americans were massacred, and where I had daily lessons on the tennis courts every summer.

According to my grandfather, this was what a well-bred young man did, along with sailing and ignoring the twentieth century.

Not terribly surprising that I tend to think of masculinity itself as a type of minor catastrophe.

In the dream, my mission was to find and lock the last door to New England in Maine so that we would be safe. (Discounting the hordes of weird and bony moose.)

I imagine this Yankee relationship with the land—formal, mythic, futile—is what drove my grandfather to wear a tie when he pulled up lobster traps in his rowboat.

# VI. conjecture

In the summer, a month before I meet N., I walk home from the store in a city known for its trees.

The students are gone, and the depopulated streets are exquisitely cautious with emptiness.

The golden afternoon light is elegiac and simple—the drugged amber of an idyll. The interlude of the wounded king, the tubercular cough, the last harvest before the endgame starts.

It makes me realize that the Vikings really had a handle on sadness, even if the only way they could deal with it was by being continuously drunk in the afterlife.

This sentiment seems more poignant because I have just purchased porn.

At dusk, alone together in the apartment overlooking the overcast Gulf, N. plays the *Moonlight Sonata* for me.

She loves Beethoven, even though people dismiss him as bombastic, because he basically invented the bass notes.

No one before him used those lower registers for anything other than counterpoint or rhythm.

The left hand kept the time, and the right hand provided the action. The left was prosaic, the right lyrical.

With Beethoven, either hand could tell the story.

This will be the only time I ever see her touch the piano. Performing took all the joy out of it for her.

Afterward, I hug her and say that it was amazing.

She smiles sadly. *Thanks. But as Thornton Wilder said, we are all equally distant from the sun.*

Had sex yesterday. Was puzzled by the fact that N. didn't try to stop me right before she came, like she usually does.

She got up to make tea, leaving me alone as I stared at the basil plant in the window radiating opulent, uncaring emerald.

Felt so fabulously dizzy and great that it was painful. Alarmed that the pain seemed to be the only thing that made it possible.

A. says her father put a penny in a jar on the dresser every time he and his wife made love.

After their first year of marriage, the jar was halfway full. It took him the rest of his life to make it to the top. A terrible argument for—and against—infinity.

N.'s math professor had the uncanny ability to instantly calculate whether or not a number was wondrous.

If you divide it by two when it's even, and multiply it by three when odd and add one, a wondrous number will eventually reach 1.

There is an unproven conjecture out there that all numbers are wondrous.

*He said such lovely things,* she told me, *but he also tore off his shirt and tie once in class because we didn't do the assignment. It was like whoever cared the most lost.*

My dad shows me his journal
entry from the year before I was born.

The one where I came to him
in a dream and said that I would be
a writer, that I would be delivered
two weeks early, that I would be a
C-section, and that there would be
no blood.

All of which came true, even the
blood. The doctor was amazed.

I've kept this in so you know that
I can't be trusted. Right?

My mother tries to convince me not to leave N. by enlisting the Jehovah's Witnesses, with whom she has been flirting. *They understand about mysteries,* she says. *About what draws people together.*

*Well, what I understand,* I say, *is that they have incorrectly predicted the end of the world sixteen times.*

She gets angry. *So you're going to be just like your father, who didn't think we should be a family? Is that what you want?*

I barely refrain from pointing out that even though he was the one who filed, she *chose* to get divorced. He wasn't going to leave her.

That is, until he discovered that the only thing that was more exciting for her than secretly having sex with a drug dealer who didn't speak any English was refusing to stop when she was caught.

It couldn't just be a mistake. It had to be a story.

Working late. N. calls drunkenly from the bar. Her coworker wants know if I am turned on by lesbians.

The only thing N. will say about losing her virginity was that it happened with two other girls. So I think I know *what* she wants me to tell him, but not *why*.

I should be angry with her, but I'm irritated at him instead. It's a rhetorical question. What doesn't turn us on? He knows as well as I do that one has to go down to the molecular level to escape the male gaze.

Also, hasn't anyone figured out by now that watching two girls together might be irresistible to men for the simple fact that the other person might actually know what they're doing?

Galen held that in order for a woman to conceive, she must achieve orgasm.

Using this logic, if you got pregnant from a rape, you must have enjoyed it, and therefore consented in the first place. Making it not a rape.

This Roman belief is what gave rise to a flurry of Victorian property law. They were worried about social climbing: that women would be forced to marry their lower-class rapists and give them their dowries. This is why they were not allowed to own anything.

Mind you, the Victorians also tried to claim that the rampant prostitution in the streets was just an epidemic of nymphomania. The poor dears.

Hosting an introductory din-
ner party for our two families.
Fought with N. over the seasonal
appropriateness of the dishes.

Feel like a fifties housewife
tamping down the jitters with Valium.

My brother tries to convince me
that the quail is not arid. I tell myself
that the rosemary mashed potatoes
make up for it.

Talking in a circle after dinner,
I recount how I named musicals for
an hour and N. could sing a line from
each one of them.

N.'s dateless sister looks up from
the sickly triangle of her over-sweet
cosmopolitan and bursts out: *Oh, my
God! You are sooo boring!*

Silence. My face burns. If I were
wearing a dress, this would definitely
be the time to flounce out of here.

# VII. storied

Visiting N.'s friend, who is manic
and disquietingly translucent.

N. says that it's because, in
college, she gave birth to a baby
with no brain. She has never quite
recovered.

So I'm not prepared for her
bragging about how she stuck with a
guy for six months because the way he
drove her Corvette made her climax
in the passenger seat.

The friend and I go to the store
for groceries in this storied vehicle,
and she mentions that she is always
insanely jealous of N.'s lovers, except
for me. She waits for me to respond.

N. thinks my universe falls apart
due to thermodynamics: karma does
not add up.

*If everyone's being reborn all the
time, then where do the new souls come
from?* She leans back, satisfied.

I imagine the type of occult
accountant who could come up with
this total. Then think of Pythagoras:
*Number is the ruler of forms and ideas
and the cause of gods and daemons.* I
love these cross-century squabbles.

The morning after N. sleeps with me for the first time, I sneak out to the grocery store to get breakfast.

I don't know her very well, so I buy two fruit tarts, two éclairs, four kiwis, a carton of raspberries, three kinds of yogurt, and a rose.

The cashier takes it all in. *Um. Either she was really good, or you were really bad.*

Chandler certainly knew how to be alone. The best parts of his books are where the hero just hangs out in his office being metaphysically bored. The prose is at its most vibrant and alive then.

But you can't trust his analogies: *Alcohol is like love. . . . The first kiss is magic, the second is intimate, the third is routine. After that you take the girl's clothes off.*

Don't mistake this for language. This is a blueprint. You don't poison ideas with arguments—you poison them with diagrams.

I am supposed to write an invocation for a friend of N.'s who is getting married. We fight over my draft for hours. It is not, she says, about them, about love.

I talk about the Curies distilling seven tons of pitcheblende in order to get a tenth of a gram of radium. How they lived in poverty in an unheated shack and had to take turns stirring the slag with a heavy iron bar for hours. But they were happy together.

I leave out the part where Marie dies from having blithely carried radioactive vials around in her coat pocket.

She kept test tubes of the stuff in her desk and loved the pretty blue-green light it gave off in the dark.

The tenser things get, the more N. wants a kid. But we might have to adopt, because of my bad genes: alcoholism, schizophrenia, depression . . . the whole sick crew.

Maybe we could go to Ireland. N. brightens up. *But we'd have to raise her Catholic.*

Every time I consider explaining to N. which parts of this I find upsetting, I envision putting a gun to my head and exploding my cranium. In a cartoonish fashion, but still.

The college graduate I first met—who wore pearls with an ankh, valorized James Bond films and performance artists with scrolled manifestoes in their pussies—is almost gone.

I find myself in the strange position of trying to protect the kid I don't want from white-knuckling it behind a picket fence.

My mother sends me a care package with ineffective oven mitts, prunes, a tiny measuring tape, yeast, dried seaweed, cheap pens, and index cards. This list has never varied during the past 20 years.

I almost call her up and say, *I'm 34. I've had sex with multiple women, I've done drugs, and you're giving me index cards. You know, for that math quiz, or my presentation on Roman numerals.*

Cleaning out the closet at
twilight, N. pauses: *Damn it. Just how
many pairs of handcuffs do we own?*

N. and I are discussing the perfected female body and whether or not pleasure is inversely proportionate to form.

I think of the early Islamic scholars and mystics who invented the idea of the *houri*.

Namely, a woman who is hairless (except for the eyebrows and head), who does not menstruate, urinate, or defecate, and is transparent right down to the marrow of her bones, *like red wine in a white glass.*

N. tries to end the discussion by declaring, *I just want to be a Barbie that is capable of orgasm.*

I laugh. Then realize that I am suddenly very angry, though I'm not sure on whose behalf.

# VIII. synonyms

N. was a champion debater, which is why I know that, under Parliamentary rules, you can heckle the opposition.

Her local debate team's hero was the philosopher Sidney Morganbesser, who had the perfect sarcastic response to the argument that there were many cases in which two negatives made a positive but none where two positives made a negative: *Yeah, yeah.*

I have never been more attracted to her than when she told me this story.

S. refuses the label of a *golden lesbian*. Not only has she touched men, she quite enjoyed having sex with them.

My poetry professor used to say that there was no such thing as a synonym. I still believe in them, but not the way I used to.

I'm sad, so I go alone to the candlelight mass at Christmas. My favorite part is the end, when the sexton brings down the lights, and I'm alone with the feeling of breathing in a dark building with hundreds of people.

I think of the Secret Gospel of Mark, the one with the verses where Lazarus falls in love with Jesus after being raised.

He spends the night alone with him, dressed only in a linen cloth, so that Jesus can teach him *the mystery of God's domain*. I reach for N.'s absent hand in the pitch black.

O. has learned how to do one
thing lyrically and to do it very well,
though narrowly.

But there are no people in his
poems, just a sensibility.

Told N.'s mother I wanted to be DNR. No resuscitation under any circumstances.

I am a fatalist. Plus, I don't want someone else to decide that I'm okay with my quality of life being less than that of the average houseplant.

She found this very distressing. Not because she is a doctor but because, as she said, *we've invested a lot in you.*

I spent the rest of the dinner in silence, thinking about the awkward bliss of zombies.

Despite being a little spastic, they're generally very relaxed and don't have to talk to anyone.

I tell S. I'm a little worried that I'll become an alcoholic if I stay with N.

Hard to avoid the constant pressure to drink heavily whenever we visit her family.

All those hours spent staring across the table at each other over endless glasses of wine.

Getting buzzed and trying to remember during the long pauses in conversation not to let anything slip that might reveal that N. dated women exclusively in college.

There's also the attractive prospect of using it as a form of vengeful performance art.

Of course, sitting down during the Fourth of July picnic with the one family friend in AA and aggressively interviewing him about the founder, Bill W., and his *nameless squad of drunks* probably already qualifies as such.

Argue with F. about the poem where the speaker can't sleep with her husband without thinking of the Ecuadorian woman with her head beaten in by paramilitaries.

F. thinks this is a virtuous, writerly act. I just feel sad for the poet's husband. Sex shouldn't be social work.

On the other hand, you don't want to turn into Thomas Mann. When we dropped the bomb on Hiroshima, his entire diary entry for that day consisted of how satisfied and happy he was about the very nice pair of shoes he had just bought.

I think of this whenever someone tries to argue that writers are more sensitive—that they *feel* more than other people.

N. says her therapist is pissed at her because she doesn't cry. She is proud of this.

I think back to my writing workshops, where I was often tempted to write the following on the more clunky avant-garde poems:

*Great. You've successfully frustrated my expectations as a reader. This is* exactly *what I go to literature for: self-referential failure.*

The sexual optimism that comes front-loaded with a Y chromosome is virtually impossible to dampen.

You don't think it will happen— you don't even *want* it to happen— yet you go around prepping for it all the same. It's humiliating.

# IX. ninjas

We're outside on the lawn at a neighbor's extravagant birthday party with N.'s family.

Her father's irritated that he's not the center of attention, so there's more than the usual amount of maintenance drinking.

N. wonders aloud where they're hiding the good stuff. Her father snorts: *Don't be a fucking moron. There is no good stuff.*

N.'s eyes shine with tears, and she looks away, pretending to stare at the derelict ice sculpture melting into the shrimp.

I realize that my fists are rising from my sides, and I stop them.

N. threatens to sue me for
*premeditation* and *mental cruelty* if I
don't sign the documents she wants
me to sign. It's almost flattering. Like
my mustache comes with a death ray.

R. says, *I find it funny that she
defines not getting everything she wants
as mental cruelty.*

I go to visit Z. in New York, and he takes me to the exhibit of flayed plastic bodies. Their careful poses make them look ambivalent despite their martyrdom.

Z. is concerned by how puffy I am. I have to get up at 5 a.m., but N. doesn't want to go to bed early. So I've been sleep deprived for six years.

We lean against the railing and look at the sheen of the beautifully poisoned river. *Look,* he says, *I love you, but she's a bully. Her tits have got nothing to do with it.*

My dad discloses that he actually briefly succeeded in dragging my mother to couples counseling.

After their time was up, the therapist announced, with peculiar intensity, *The men's bathroom is down the hall to the right.*

As my dad was returning, the therapist slipped out and intercepted him in the corridor.

*I shouldn't be doing this,* he said. *It's not even professional. But that woman in there just wants a house and money, and she wants you to take care of everything.*

He paused meaningfully. They looked at each other.

Generally, men bore me, but I have to admire this moment. We may not be able to approximate an honest emotion, but damned if we can't float an implication.

Z. helps me look past the long conversation wherein I will attempt to explain to N. that experiencing a crippling orgasm of fury when it comes time to apologize is fatal, romantically speaking.

*All you have to do,* he says, *is utter these things calmly, look at her out of slitted eyes, and then vanish. Like a ninja.*

I am not comforted. Where will I go? Am I going to be one of those divorced people with an empty loft?

Z. shakes his head. *Don't be silly. Ninjas don't need furniture.*

x. what watch?

N. reveals in couples therapy that she went off birth control three months ago.

As if she had actually told me that she was no longer taking her pills.

She says it with such a lack of emphasis that it takes me a moment.

Then the room becomes bright and horribly detailed.

I prepare a script for the talk, but it doesn't help. N. grabs a colorless bottle of pinot grigio and slams the bedroom door behind her. There's weeping, but I can't hear it.

I sit all night in the recliner, motionless. It's like waiting for a death.

I keep thinking of her favorite lines from *Casablanca*, where a smuggled German couple attempts to tell time in an American way:

*Liebchen—uh . . . sweetness heart . . . What watch?*

*Ten watch.*

*Such watch?*

This shorthand makes them encrypted, and alone, in a way that nothing else can.

The sweetness of the contract in this scene is the only thing that stands in the way of the agonizing impulse I have every other minute to rush through the door and comfort her. If I move, it will be lost.

Go out with X. to the redwoods. They're so massive that I have no trouble imagining why druids worshipped trees.

One has fallen beside the path, and we climb onto the trunk. X. starts taking pictures.

I hunker down in the shafts of mathematical light coming through the trees and read the graffiti: Z_+DL ALW__Z.

I don't know why I love the omissions. They make me want to go back, to fix the asterisks other people carved over them.

However brief it is, this foreshortened equation is still—like everything else in the universe—made up of names.

I start crying. Not in a thoughtful or becoming way. In an ugly way. In a way that only has one purpose.

X. takes shot after shot of me. I don't look up. Before I knelt down, I thought slyly that it might make a nice author photograph. Now it will be something other.

After swimming, E. and I drive through the calm oaks on either side of the back road.

We stop at a gourmet grocery set randomly beside a field, buy pomegranates and dark chocolate, and sit down at the edge of the parking lot. Watch the effortless light on the tall grass, the sun going down.

E. talks about the Masons, theoretical particles, her new love. What they do and don't have to do with each other.

I say nothing, which makes me suspect that I am happy.

N. would never let me kiss or lick the small serif on the side of her breast where they removed the mass. It was neither benign nor malignant. Simply anomalous.

I liked it because it made me think of the Japanese art of *kintsugi*. When a work of ceramic broke, they would inlay the cracks with gold, and find it more beautiful afterward, because it existed in time now and had a history.

E. reads the foregoing. Says I'd better be grinning on the back cover in psychedelic plaid and a beanie.

I imagine myself standing in front of a mushroom cloud, looking engaged: *Q. lives near the crater with his two mutants and what used to be a cat.*

There are many endings. Most of them atomic. This is one.

# Acknowledgments

Sections from *Monograph* first appeared in the following publications and are reprinted here with thanks: *5 AM, AGNI, Arts & Letters, decomP, Gulf Coast, Hotel Amerika, Hoot, Notre Dame Review, Salamander,* and *Sentence.*

Thanks to Denise Duhamel for seeing the shape of this chimera; to Bethany Snead and Jon Davies for their professionalism and acumen; to the University of Georgia Press for holding a place in their magnificent array of books; and to Stephanie Stio, the editors and funders of the National Poetry Series, and the Lannan Foundation for their stunning commitment to poetry.

# Credits

## II

"The first image he told me . . ." Chris Marker, *Sans Soleil* (1983; New York: Criterion Collection, 2007), DVD.

"I became a criminal . . ." Louise Gluck, "Siren," *Meadowlands* (New York: Ecco, 1997).

## III

"Man and woman were given . . ." Sherry Simon, *Gender in Translation* (New York: Routledge, 1996).

"sense of living one's deepest . . ." Joan Didion, *The White Album* (New York: Farrar, Straus and Giroux, 1979).

"There is no God of Israel . . ." Dion Fortune, *What Is Occultism?* (York Beach, Maine: Weiser, 2001).

## IV

"If it's true that there are but . . ." Clark Glymour, *Theory and Evidence* (Princeton, N.J.: Princeton University Press, 1980).

"about as mystical as a sofa" Philip Levine, *Don't Ask* (Ann Arbor: University of Michigan Press, 1981).

## V

"There are some people I know . . ." Leonard Cohen, *Greatest Hits* (1975; Weybridge: Sony UK, 2009), CD.

## VI

"we are all equally distant from the sun." Thornton Wilder, *The Selected Letters of Thornton Wilder*, edited by Jackson R. Bryer and Robin Gibbs (New York: HarperCollins, 2009).

## VII

"Number is the ruler of forms..." *Iamblichus' Life of Pythagoras*, translated by Thomas Taylor (1818; Rochester, Vt.: Inner Traditions, 1986).

"Alcohol is like love..." Raymond Chandler, *The Long Goodbye* (1953; New York: Vintage, 1988).

"like red wine in a white glass" Marvin Yakos, *Jesus, Jews and Jihad* (Maitland, Fla.: Xulon Press, 2006).

## VIII

"the mystery of God's domain" *The Complete Gospels: Annotated Scholar's Version*, edited by Robert J. Miller, 4th ed. (Salem, Oreg.: Polebridge Press, 2010).

## X

"Liebchen—uh . . . sweetness heart . . ." Michael Curtiz, *Casablanca* (1942; Burbank, Calif.: Warner Home Video, 2010), DVD.